THE OPTIMISTIC TEEN

YOU DON'T HAVE TO ACE EVERY TEST TO SHINE; SOMETIMES, ALL YOU NEED IS A LITTLE OPTIMISM.

VIRIKA GARG

To the students,

Who feel unseen, unheard, or unsure—this is for you.

You don't have to ace every test to shine; sometimes, all you need is a little optimism.

Here's to believing in yourself, on the bright side of every challenge,

And in the power of small, daily wins.

Keep going—your story is just beginning.

Contents

Acknowledgements

Writing this book has been a journey of reflection, growth, and quiet discovery — one I didn't even realize I was on until I reached the final page.

First and foremost, I extend my deepest gratitude *To my Mummy, Shilpa Garg.* Your unwavering support, belief in me, and quiet encouragement gave me the strength to start — and finish — something I once thought was too big for someone my age.

To my Papa, Mukesh Garg. Your steadfast support — combined with your legendary scoldings (better known as "inspirational taunts") — was the unexpected driving force behind this book's completion. Thank you for always believing in me, in your own wonderfully unique way.

To my Bhai — my partner-in-chaos and my constant cheerleader — Devyansh Garg (Chiku), thank you for reminding me to take breaks and laugh.

To my Family — thank you for being my strongest foundation. Your love, support, and silent strength have shaped more than just these pages — you've shaped the person behind them.

To my Friends — from near and far — even though you had no idea I was writing this, your kindness, your stories, and your everyday optimism found their way into these pages.

To my Teachers, across the schools I've studied in — thank you for being the silent architects behind my thoughts. Whether it was the way you explained life during a lesson or simply believed in me beyond grades, your influence echoes in every chapter.

*This book may carry my name on the cover, but it carries
all of you in its heart.*

Preface

Hey there! I'm excited that you're holding this book in your hands because what you're about to read is not just about school or grades—it's about something much bigger: *your journey as a student.* Whether you're labelled as an *"average"* student or a *"topper"*, this book is for you, and trust me, I know both sides of the coin.

Now, I'm not here to tell you grades don't matter. They do, especially when it comes to exams that can shape your future. If you're a student like me, you've probably felt the pressure that comes with exams, and expectations, and yes, those moments when people just want to know, *"How much did you score?"* I get it—entrance exams, boards, the constant rush to prove yourself—it can be a lot!   But tell me one thing: *Will stressing out about your grades help you achieve better ones?* Of course, no right? You simply can't let the fear of failure control you. Instead, what you can do is focus on the *process of learning.* The grades will follow naturally if you're truly engaged with what you're studying.

So yes, work hard, and aim high, but also *don't lose yourself* in the race for marks. Understand that every test, every subject, and every challenge is part of a bigger picture. It's part of your growth, your learning curve, and your story.

Now, if you are thinking, what made me write this book?

Well, I wrote this book because I've been in your shoes. One day you're celebrated for doing well, and the next, if your marks slip, people start wondering what went wrong.

It's like always being judged by the numbers on a piece of paper. And let me tell you, as someone who has changed schools *nine times* (yes, you read that right!), I've experienced all sorts of environments, teachers, and students. I've been in schools where I was the new kid struggling to fit in, and others where I felt at the top of my game. But through all those changes, the only thing that stayed with me was the *power of optimism*.

Changing schools so many times gave me a unique perspective. I've seen how different students cope with pressure—some thrive, some struggle, but what truly made the difference wasn't just their intelligence or marks. It was their mindset. That's why I believe that having an optimistic mindset is essential.

I know first-hand that student life can be overwhelming, and sometimes, it feels like there's no way out of the stress. But through my experience, I've come to realize something important: **optimism is a superpower**. I know, I know, I have been repeating this, that Optimism is very important... but why?? Why is it so important?? Optimism allows you to stay grounded when everything feels uncertain. It reminds you that while this one test might seem like the most important thing right now, there's a bigger journey ahead. It tells you that it's okay not to excel every single time.

Studies even show that optimistic students tend to handle stress better and are more resilient in the face of setbacks. When you approach challenges with an optimistic mindset, you're not as easily shaken by failure. You bounce back, you learn, and you keep going. And that's the mindset I want you to embrace as you read this book.

As I mentioned earlier, I've changed schools nine times. That's nine different sets of teachers, students, rules, and environments! And you know what? It was tough at times, but it also taught me so much about resilience, adaptation, and yes, optimism. Every new school came with its own challenges, but it also came with new opportunities to learn—about others and about myself.

In each new place, I met students who were "toppers" and students who were "average," but one thing I learned from all of them is that success isn't just about how smart you are or how high your marks are, it's about how you handle the ups and downs. It's about staying positive even when things don't go your way. This constant change in my life showed me that optimism can help you adjust, grow, and thrive in any situation.

This book isn't about being a perfect student. It's about embracing the fact that *none of us are perfect*, and that's *perfectly* fine. It's about taking control of your mindset and using optimism to push through the tough times. Whether you're preparing for an important exam, dealing with the pressure to always be on top, or just trying to find your footing in the chaos of school life, I hope this book will guide you.

I'm not just speaking from theory—I've lived it. I've been the *new kid*. I've been the *average student*. I've been the *topper*. And through it all, I've tried to be an *optimistic student*. It's the key to keeping your head up, no matter what comes your way.

So whether you're a student who feels like no one notices your efforts or someone who's tired of the pressure to always be perfect, this book is here to remind you that it's okay to be human. It's okay to have ups and downs. What's more important is how you respond to those moments with optimism. So, welcome to this journey! By the time you reach the end of this book, I hope you'll feel empowered to take on your challenges with a fresh, optimistic mindset.

CHAPTER ONE

THE POWER OF PERSPECTIVE

*"Optimism is the one quality
more associated with success and happiness than any
other."*

– Brian Tracy

Introduction to Optimism

Sometimes, I feel we live in a world full of expectations. Have you ever felt like your report card weighs more than the actual learning you've done? Or like the score on a test somehow speaks louder than all the effort you put in? It doesn't matter if you're a "*topper*" or an "*average*" student—there's this pressure that surrounds you, right?

Talking about those labels we get stuck with...
If you're an average student, you might have heard this a million times: "*You need to improve. Push yourself harder!*" It's like no matter how hard you're already trying, you're expected to keep climbing, even if the hill feels impossibly steep.

And then, if you're a topper, it can look like you've got it easy. But really, it's complicated, isn't it? There's this constant pressure to stay perfect, and if you slip even a little, the question isn't *"Did you do your best?"* but *"What went wrong?"* I remember once when I got my report card. I had done pretty well in most subjects, but one of my scores wasn't great. It wasn't that bad, but you know, it was *"average."* Instead of hearing *"Good job!"* for the other subjects, all I got was, *"You really need to focus more on that particular subject next time."* Sound familiar? It's like all your other achievements vanish into thin air because one subject didn't go as planned.

Take this moment to think about your own experiences. Maybe it was a test, a sports match, or even a hobby. How did you feel when all anyone noticed was what went wrong? Did it make you want to keep going or give up?

Why Optimism Matters

Now here's the big question: *What do we do about all this pressure?*

We can't escape everyone's expectations—teachers, parents, and sometimes even our own—but we can change the way we see things. *How?* **Enter optimism.** No, I'm not talking about some fluffy, "think happy thoughts" vibe. I mean a practical mindset shift that can change how you see yourself and your potential, no matter what your report card says.

Think about Kung Fu Panda's Po. He didn't start as a skilled warrior. Far from it! But Po had optimism—he believed that he could become the Dragon Warrior, even when others doubted him. His mindset helped him grow into the role, step by step.

And remember Dory from Finding Nemo? She didn't have all the answers, but her unwavering belief in "just keep swimming" kept her moving forward. Optimism didn't make Dory's journey easy, but it made it possible.

Remember in Harry Potter when Ron drinks the Felix Felicis (the lucky potion) before a Quidditch match? Suddenly, everything goes perfectly for him. But guess what? Harry hadn't actually given him the potion! That's optimism. It's not about a magic spell; it's about your mindset.

This mindset can work in your life, too. Optimism isn't just hoping things will get better; it's believing they can get better *if you're willing to take action.*

How Optimism Works

You've probably been told to "think positively" when facing stressful exams or worrying about your performance. While optimism does involve positive thinking, it's actually much more than that—it's about having a *growth mindset*. This mindset is based on the belief that your abilities can be improved with time, effort, and persistence. As a student, optimism can be one of your greatest strengths, helping you handle challenges more effectively and keep going when things get tough.

Let's face it: school life can be overwhelming. Between exams, assignments, friendships, and balancing a packed schedule, there are bound to be moments when you feel like you're falling short—either of your own expectations or those set by others. But optimism can change how you approach these moments. It allows you to see challenges as opportunities for growth rather than as failures. In fact, if you think about it, most people who succeed aren't just lucky or naturally talented; they're persistent. And it's optimism that fuels their persistence, helping them keep pushing forward.

Optimism isn't just about hoping for the best—*it actively drives your effort. When you believe that a better outcome is possible, you're more likely to take practical steps to make it happen.* For example, if you're struggling with a particular subject, an optimistic mindset can encourage you to seek help, study more consistently, and practice until you improve. A person with an optimistic mindset says, "*I may not be able to control every situation, but I can control the effort I put in.*" And that's what makes optimism so powerful: it transforms hope into action, motivating you to keep going, even when it's hard.

Optimism also affects your brain in a surprisingly powerful way. Research shows that maintaining a positive outlook actually changes brain chemistry. When you approach situations with optimism, your brain releases chemicals that help you stay focused, motivated, and resilient. This makes it easier to manage stress effectively. Of course, optimism doesn't mean you won't feel anxious or overwhelmed at times; those feelings are natural. But an optimistic mindset helps you deal with them in a constructive way. Instead of getting bogged down by fear and doubt, optimism enables you to make clearer decisions and stay calmer under pressure. It's almost like a mental boost that helps you think and act more effectively just when you need it most.

Here's a common misunderstanding: *real optimism isn't about blindly believing everything will work out just because you want it to.* There's something called **complacent optimism**—it's like waiting around, expecting good things to happen *without* putting in effort. Ever thought, "It'll be fine" and then been disappointed when things didn't magically get better? *That's complacent optimism.*

But **conditional optimism**? Now, that's where the real power lies. It's thinking, "I believe things can improve *if* I work for it." Imagine you want to build a treehouse. With conditional optimism, you say, *"If I gather some wood, nails, and get a few friends to help, we can make this happen."* **Conditional optimism means action.** You believe in positive outcomes, but you're also ready to work for them. That's the mindset that drives *real progress.* It's that inner voice that says, **"You've got this,"** when self-doubt creeps in. It's not about being unrealistic; it's about choosing hope over fear, especially in moments when the future seems uncertain.

As I said earlier, I didn't always have the highest grades in every subject, however, I learned to focus on *what I could improve rather than what others thought I should achieve.* Instead of stressing over what went wrong, I tried to approach each new challenge as an opportunity to grow. And that's what optimism is about—it's *a mindset that helps you keep going, even when things don't go your way.* I understood that what matters more than meeting every expectation is how you handle the pressure. And when you approach life with optimism, you start to realize that each challenge, each test, and even each failure is part of your learning experience. Your worth isn't defined by a single mark or grade—it's defined by how you grow, adapt, and keep moving forward. It's not about blind hope or always thinking positive. It's about choosing to believe that your struggles aren't permanent—that they're part of the process. Whether you're a topper or an average student, you're going to face setbacks. You're going to feel pressure from teachers, parents, friends, and even from yourself. Optimism isn't about ignoring that pressure; it's about finding the strength to face it head-on.

The real test of optimism comes during challenging times. It's easy to be optimistic when life is smooth, but optimism is most valuable when life throws obstacles your way. When you're overwhelmed by schoolwork, personal stress, or uncertainty about the future, optimism becomes your anchor—it keeps you grounded, reminding you that tough times are temporary, and you have the resilience to push through.

For me, constantly moving from school to school was one of the hardest challenges I faced. Switching schools wasn't easy for me. Each time, I had to adjust to new people, new environments, and, of course, new academic standards. I remember how much I used to cry, feeling lost and frustrated. It wasn't just about adapting to new syllabi—some schools followed ICSE, others CBSE—it was about feeling like I was always starting from scratch, while others were building their lives in one place. I even felt angry at my parents, wondering why I couldn't just stay in one school like everyone else. Each new school came with a fresh set of people, unfamiliar environments, and new academic expectations, which left me feeling like I was always at a disadvantage.

But as hard as it was, there came a moment when I realized that no matter how much I cried or wished things were different, I couldn't turn back time. I couldn't redo my grades or stay in one place just to feel comfortable. It was then that I had to make a choice—keep focusing on what I had lost or change the way I saw the situation. It wasn't easy, but I decided to think differently, to embrace the constant change, and focus on what I could control—my own growth, and my attitude.

It was optimism that helped me through those times.

Instead of being overwhelmed by the fear of starting over again, I started to see each new school as a new opportunity. And while I may not have had perfect grades or years to build long-lasting friendships, something unexpected happened—I began to make a positive impact in those short moments. Teachers and friends I met for just a year or two still remember me, not because of my marks, but because of the person I was. I'm still in touch with some of them, and those friendships and memories have become some of the most meaningful parts of my life.

I realized that it wasn't about being perfect or excelling all the time—it was about the connections I made and the resilience I built along the way. And looking back now, I see how optimism helped me to stop focusing on what was missing and start appreciating what I was gaining.

This experience taught me something invaluable: that tough times don't last, but the way we face them does. And when you approach those moments with optimism, you not only survive them, you grow from them.

The nervousness, the first-day jitters—all of it was part of the learning curve. If I had stayed stuck in the mindset of "I'll never fit in," I would've missed out on the chance to learn resilience. Every change taught me something valuable, and that's optimism in action. So remember, optimism isn't about ignoring the struggle; it's about recognizing the strength you gain from it.

Let's bring this together. Whether you're a topper or an average student, the struggles you face are more similar than you think. The weight of expectations, the fear of disappointing others, and the pressure to prove yourself—these are things all students deal with. And that's why optimism is so important. Know that optimism can be your best friend. It helps you see past the grades, the expectations, and the pressure, and focus on what really matters: your growth, your learning, and your journey. It helps us step back, take a deep breath, and realize that we're not defined by one test, one performance, or one moment. It reminds us to keep our heads up, to stay hopeful, and to keep learning, no matter what.

Remember, you're more than just a number on a report card. You're a student with a story, with ups and downs, successes and failures. When the pressure feels too heavy, when you feel like you're being pulled in every direction, let optimism guide you. Because in the end, it's not about meeting every expectation—*it's about learning, growing, and staying hopeful.*

Let's pause for a moment. Think about your current challenges. Maybe it's school, friendships, or learning something new. Write down one challenge you're facing and ask yourself:

- What can I control in this situation?
- What small step can I take to make it better?

This simple exercise can be your starting point. Optimism is like building a muscle—you strengthen it with practice. So, I challenge you: take one small step toward optimism today. Choose hope. Choose growth. Choose to "just keep swimming," even when the waters feel rough.

CHAPTER TWO

FINDING THE LIGHT

"A pessimist is one who makes difficulties of his opportunities and an optimist is one who makes opportunities of his difficulties."

– Harry S. Truman

What if the way we interpret our challenges could make all the difference between giving up and pushing forward? Imagine two students, each facing a similar setback but viewing it in very different ways. Their stories reveal how mindset—whether optimistic, or pessimistic —can shape not only their responses but also their outcomes.

Meet Student 1, who recently received a disappointing grade on an important project. Instead of feeling defeated, they think, "This is tough, but I can learn from it and do better next time. Maybe this is a chance to improve." Motivated by growth, they quickly start planning how to study differently for the next exam. Their setback becomes fuel for their drive to improve.

Student 2, however, reacts differently. They see the low grade and think, "I knew it. No matter how hard I try, it's never good enough. Why put in more effort if this is all I get?" Feeling disheartened, they stop studying altogether, convinced that trying won't change anything.

When we look at these responses, it becomes clear how powerful optimism can be. Student 1's optimistic outlook turns setbacks into stepping stones. By choosing to see obstacles as opportunities, they're setting themselves up for long-term growth. Student 2's pessimism, on the other hand, leads them to give up altogether, missing out on the possibility of improvement.

Reflecting on the Optimistic Student (The Can-do Attitude Squad):

The *optimistic student* approaches challenges with a growth mindset. They understand that setbacks aren't failures; they're just steps in the learning process. When faced with a lower-than-expected test grade, instead of spiralling into self-doubt, the optimistic student sees it as feedback. They ask themselves, "What can I improve on for next time?" and immediately start planning their next steps. This mindset keeps them motivated, resilient, and more likely to try new things—even if they're challenging.

Optimistic students don't just stop at effort; they believe that effort leads to *improvement*. When stress arises, they handle it with resilience, seeing it as part of the journey to success rather than as a roadblock. Their mindset allows them to focus on *progress, not perfection*.

-<u>Optimistic Student Traits</u>:

- Views setbacks as valuable learning experiences.

- Believes that with effort, they can improve.

- Is resilient under pressure and motivated to try hard things.

- Faces challenges with curiosity and openness to growth.

Reflecting on the Pessimistic Student (The Why Bother? Club):

On the other hand, *the pessimistic student* often feels defeated before they even begin. They tend to view failures as reflections of their abilities or worth, rather than as opportunities for learning. When this student doesn't perform well, their first thought might be, "No matter what I do, I can't succeed." This belief discourages them from putting in effort because they're convinced it won't make a difference.

This mindset can also harm mental health, increasing stress and making it harder to bounce back from setbacks. It's not that the pessimistic student isn't capable—they're simply held back by their own doubts, which prevent them from fully engaging with their potential.

-<u>Pessimistic Student Traits</u>:

- Sees failures as proof of their limitations.

- Believes that effort is pointless and won't change outcomes.

- Avoids challenges to escape potential disappointment.

- Struggles with stress, often feeling defeated by obstacles.

In the end, optimism stands out as the mindset most likely to lead to success. Why? Because an optimistic student doesn't just see things as they are—they also see what could be. This mindset encourages them to push forward, learn from setbacks, and stay motivated, even when challenges arise.

Finding Balance with Realism:

We've explored how optimism and pessimism shape responses to challenges, but there's a third approach we haven't discussed yet: **realism**. This perspective can be valuable in its own way, as it focuses on seeing things as they are, without the ups and downs of optimism or pessimism. Let's look at how a **realistic student** approaches challenges and see why, even with its strengths, realism lacks the forward momentum that optimism offers.

Student 3: The Realistic Approach (The Play It Safe Approach)

Student 3, our realist, is practical and objective. When they receive a disappointing grade, they don't react too emotionally; instead, they think, "I did my best, and this is how it turned out. There are things I could have done differently, but what's done is done." They accept the grade as it is without a strong emotional response, and while they might make minor adjustments, they don't invest in any major changes.

This balanced mindset helps Student 3 avoid intense disappointment, but it also means they may miss opportunities for growth. By focusing only on what is, rather than what could be, a realist might become complacent or stagnant. They avoid the highs and lows but also lack the drive to push themselves to the next level.

-<u>Realistic Student Traits</u>:

-Accepts situations as they are, without overanalyzing or emotional reactions.

-Stays balanced and avoids extreme reactions to successes or setbacks.

-May lack motivation to pursue higher goals or go beyond their comfort zone.

In some ways, realism seems like a middle ground, offering stability without getting too hopeful or too discouraged. But here's the real question: Isn't optimism unrealistic? Isn't it better to stick with realism and avoid disappointment altogether? In your journey through optimism, you've likely come across different outlooks among friends or classmates. While you might find optimism exciting and empowering, others might see it as ignoring reality. Take, for example, a student we'll call Siya, who prefers to stay "realistic" over "optimistic." When facing an exam, she says, "I'd rather expect the worst and be ready for it than hope for the best and end up disappointed."

You may wonder, "Isn't optimism just unrealistic? What if things actually go wrong?" Here's why that idea doesn't quite hit the mark. Realism and optimism aren't opposites; they're both ways of looking at situations, but they serve different purposes. Realism helps us see the present clearly, while optimism gives us the energy to move toward a better future.

Think of it this way: while realism points out, "Here are the challenges," optimism says, "Here's why facing those challenges is worth it." Siya's realistic mindset isn't wrong, but it may limit her by keeping her focus on potential failures rather than possible growth. Optimism doesn't ignore the real risks or struggles—it just believes in the possibility of finding solutions.

Optimism isn't about ignoring facts. It's about choosing how you respond to them. When you're optimistic, you acknowledge obstacles, but instead of giving up, you seek ways to work through them. Here's where optimism helps you:

1. Staying motivated under pressure – Instead of getting discouraged by the difficulties, optimism helps you stay engaged and willing to try, even when things are tough.

2. Turning setbacks into lessons – With optimism, failure isn't the end; it's part of the learning curve. Each setback becomes an opportunity to improve.
3. Seeing solutions, not just problems – Where pessimism might dwell on obstacles, optimism encourages you to look for possibilities. It's not about ignoring challenges but actively seeking ways to overcome them.

For example, if you're struggling in math, a realistic outlook might say, "I'm not good at this." Optimism, however, would add, "I can improve if I find the right help." Instead of lowering your expectations, optimism invites you to raise your effort.

In truth, you need both realism and optimism. Realism helps you see things clearly, but without optimism, it's easy to get stuck. Optimism without realism, on the other hand, could lead to overconfidence. So, instead of choosing one over the other, think of optimism and realism as teammates. Realism shows you where you are; optimism shows you where you could be. Together, they help you tackle challenges more effectively.

Imagine you're preparing for an exam, and you realize there's a lot you don't know. A purely realistic mindset might say, "This is hopeless," while a purely optimistic mindset might say, "I'll be fine even if I don't study." A balanced mindset would look at the challenge realistically—"I need to work on this"—and use optimism to fuel action—"If I practice consistently, I'll improve."

Ultimately, optimism isn't about ignoring difficulties; it's about believing that improvement is possible and worth striving for.

CHAPTER THREE

OPTIMISM IN SCHOOL LIFE

"True hopefulness and optimism is what leads one to dare. It is also what lifts one back up to dare again after a failed attempt."

- Bibi Bourelly

Academics have always felt like a huge part of my life, and I'm sure it's the same for most students. Think about it: out of 24 hours, we spend 7–8 hours in school, and then there's tuition, homework, and study sessions. It's like a never-ending cycle. And while some people say, "Marks don't define you," we can't deny that in today's competitive world, good marks do matter. They can open up opportunities and boost our confidence. But with this comes a lot of pressure, and let's be honest, we've all felt it at some point—especially during exams.

That's why I wanted to explore the idea of optimism in academics. I've been there too—feeling stressed out, doubting myself, or worrying about what others might think if I don't do well. And I started wondering: what if there's a better way to deal with all this? What if instead of letting the pressure get to us, we could use optimism to stay motivated and push through challenges?

First, let's dive in and see how optimism can make our academic journeys a little brighter and a lot less stressful!

The Hidden Side of Optimism in Learning

Curiosity Over Perfection:

Students who are overly focused on perfection hesitate to ask questions because they fear looking "dumb" or being judged. Optimism, however, shifts the focus from "I should already know this" to "I can learn this." It allows students to ask questions freely, leading to deeper understanding. For example, in a science class, an optimistic student might ask, "Why does a plane stay in the air?" even if it seems like a basic question. A perfectionist, afraid of judgment, might stay silent and miss out on valuable learning.

Freedom to Fail:

Optimism shifts your mindset from "I failed, so I'm not good enough" to "I failed, so I have something to learn." Instead of treating mistakes as proof of incompetence, an optimistic mindset sees them as part of the learning process. For example, imagine you bomb a math test. A pessimistic approach might make you feel like you're just "bad at math" and there's no point in trying. But an optimistic perspective helps you see the test as a diagnostic tool—it shows you where you went wrong, what needs improvement, and what strategies you can change next time.

Reframing Challenges as Adventures:

Take a difficult subject, for example—many students dread topics like math or science, but an optimistic mindset shifts the perspective. Instead of thinking, *"I'll never understand this,"* optimism helps us see it as a puzzle waiting to be solved. It sparks curiosity, making us ask, *"What if I approach this differently?"* This sense of discovery turns frustration into motivation. Just like a hero in a movie who faces obstacles before achieving success, every difficulty becomes another chapter in our personal growth. Ultimately, optimism doesn't erase the challenges of school life, but it changes how we experience them.

Seeing Beyond Grades:
A student driven by grades might cram formulas without understanding them, just to score well. However, an optimistic student sees learning as an opportunity to expand their knowledge. They focus on understanding concepts rather than just rote learning, which makes education more meaningful and enjoyable. In a competitive academic environment, students often compare their grades with others. Optimism helps break this cycle. Instead of thinking, *"I need to score higher than my friend,"* an optimistic mindset says, *"I need to improve from where I was yesterday."* This fosters personal growth rather than unhealthy competition.

Turning Pressure Into Purpose:
When students feel pressured, they often think, "I have to study for this test" or "I have to complete this assignment." This makes studying feel like a chore. However, an optimistic mindset shifts this thinking to "I want to study because it will help me grow" or "I want to do this project because it challenges me." Instead of seeing schoolwork as just an obligation, optimism helps students see the bigger picture—learning isn't just about marks; it's about developing skills, curiosity, and a sense of accomplishment.

Optimism as a Team Effort:
Optimism isn't something we have to figure out alone- it thrives in groups. Whether it's friends motivating each

other to study or teachers encouraging their students, optimism grows when we share it. A positive outlook often makes group studies more productive and fun, as we encourage each other instead of competing. Whether it's explaining a tough concept, sharing notes, or simply saying, "You'll get it next time," these small acts of support make learning easier and more enjoyable.

Reflection

In this chapter, we have explored the various ways in which optimism plays a crucial role in school life—shaping how we learn, handle challenges, and stay motivated. From shifting perspectives on grades to making learning more engaging, optimism influences academics in more ways than we often realize.

Beyond motivation and stress management, optimism has many hidden dimensions in learning. It fuels curiosity, encourages resilience, and allows us to view challenges as opportunities rather than obstacles. It helps us see beyond grades, turning learning into an engaging and fulfilling process rather than just a means to an end. Optimism is also a team effort—it flourishes in classrooms, group studies, and friendships, creating an environment where students support and uplift each other.

Of course, these are just some of the many ways optimism influences school life. The impact of a positive mindset extends far beyond what I have discussed here, but the key takeaway is clear—optimism is not just about feeling good; it is a powerful tool that shapes the way we learn, grow, and navigate the academic journey.

For now, we have discussed its impact, but the tools and techniques to cultivate optimism in school life will be explored later in the book.

Reflection Activity: Your Optimism Journal

Take a moment to reflect on your own academic journey. Optimism isn't just about thinking positively—it's about how you approach challenges, setbacks, and successes in school.

Try this:

1. **Identify a Challenge:** Think of a recent academic challenge you faced—maybe a tough test, a subject you struggle with, or a moment when you felt discouraged.
2. **Write Two Perspectives:**

   - First, describe how you initially felt about it. Did you feel frustrated? Doubtful? Unmotivated?
   - Now, rewrite that situation with an optimistic outlook. If you could go back, how would you reframe your thoughts? What could you learn from it?

3. **Action Plan:** Based on what you wrote, list one small way you can bring optimism into your studies. It could be as simple as asking for help without hesitation, viewing mistakes as learning steps, or setting a small goal to improve.

This simple reflection can help you see how shifting your mindset can make academics feel more manageable and even enjoyable. Try doing this regularly, and you might start noticing a real change in the way you approach learning!

CHAPTER FOUR

OPTIMISM IN DAILY LIFE

"Be Optimistic – People want to be around others who view life as a positive venture."

- Ace McCloud

Since we have explored different aspects of optimism in school life, it's time to see beyond the classroom walls. Life outside school is a vast, unpredictable journey filled with challenges, surprises, and opportunities. The way we perceive and respond to these experiences shapes our path.

As we step beyond school, we enter a world where learning doesn't stop but simply changes form. From personal relationships and career aspirations to health, community involvement, and even global affairs, optimism plays a vital role in shaping our approach to life. It is the force that turns obstacles into opportunities and setbacks into stepping stones. This chapter delves into how optimism influences various aspects of life beyond school and how adopting a hopeful perspective can make all the difference.

Personal Relationships: Building Bridges with Positivity

Imagine two siblings, Ria and Arjun. Ria is preparing for an important competition, but Arjun, in moment of carelessness, accidentally deletes her entire project. Furious, Mia could lash out and hold a grudge, letting resentment build between them. But instead, she takes a deep breath and chooses to believe that Arjun didn't do it intentionally. Instead of anger, she focuses on problem-solving, and together, they manage to recreate the project—stronger than before.

Optimism in relationships is not about ignoring problems but about choosing to see people with kindness, understanding, and hope. As Maya Angelou once said, *"If you find it in your heart to care for somebody else, you will have succeeded."* An optimistic approach to relationships makes conflicts easier to resolve, deepens trust, and turns mistakes into moments of growth rather than sources of division.

Career Aspirations: Seeing Possibilities, Not Limits

I remember the first time I participated in a public speaking competition. My hands were shaking, my voice wavered, and I stumbled over a few words. Walking off the stage, I felt like I hadn't done my best. But instead of dwelling on what went wrong, I focused on what I could improve. When the results were announced, I was surprised—I had secured second place. It wasn't a perfect performance, but it was proof that I was capable of more than I had thought.

This is exactly how optimism works in career aspirations. It's not about achieving instant perfection but about seeing progress, learning from every experience, and believing that setbacks don't define the future. As Steve Jobs once said, "You can't connect the dots looking forward; you can only connect them looking backward." The key is to keep moving forward, knowing that every challenge is shaping you for something bigger.

Health and Well-being: The Mind-Body Connection

Consider two athletes recovering from the same injury. One constantly worries about never being able to perform at their best again, while the other focuses on rehabilitation, trusting that with time and effort, they'll regain their strength. The second athlete not only recovers faster but also returns with a stronger mindset.

Science supports this—studies show that optimistic individuals experience lower stress levels, better immunity, and even faster recovery from illnesses. A famous example is Michael Jordan, who battled injuries throughout his career but never let setbacks define him. He once said, "Obstacles don't have to stop you. If you run into a wall, don't turn around and give up. Figure out how to climb it, go through it, or work around it."

Optimism in health isn't about ignoring struggles—it's about believing that challenges can be overcome with the right mindset and actions. Whether it's a minor cold or a major setback, a hopeful attitude makes healing—both physical and emotional—much more achievable.

Community Engagement: Spreading Hope, Creating Change

Imagine a small town struggling with frequent power cuts. Most residents complain, believing nothing can be done. But a group of young volunteers sees an opportunity—they start a campaign promoting solar energy. Slowly, more households adopt solar panels, and within a few years, the town significantly reduces its dependence on unreliable electricity. What started as a simple initiative driven by optimism led to a lasting impact on the entire community.

This is the power of optimism in community engagement. It's not about ignoring problems but believing that change is possible, even through small efforts. One great example is Malala Yousafzai, who stood up for girls' education despite immense challenges. Her unwavering belief that "One child, one teacher, one book, and one pen can change the world" has inspired millions to take action.

Whether it's volunteering, advocating for a cause, or simply helping a neighbour, optimism fuels the motivation to create a better world. A single effort might seem small, but when combined with others, it can spark a wave of meaningful change.

A Global Perspective: Finding Hope in a Chaotic World

When the COVID-19 pandemic struck, the world was overwhelmed with fear and uncertainty. Lockdowns, economic crises, and a rising death toll made it feel like an unbeatable challenge. But even in the darkest moments, scientists, healthcare workers, and communities held on to hope. Within a year, vaccines were developed—something that typically takes a decade. People supported each other, businesses adapted, and the world gradually found a way forward.

This is the essence of optimism on a global scale. It doesn't mean ignoring crises like pandemics, climate change, or conflicts—it means believing that solutions are possible and working toward them. As Desmond Tutu once said, "Hope is being able to see that there is light despite all of the darkness."

The fight against COVID-19 proved that even in the face of a global crisis, human resilience, innovation, and collaboration can lead to extraordinary breakthroughs. Challenges will always exist, but history shows that when optimism meets action, the world finds a way forward.

Life Transitions: Embracing Change with Confidence

Life is full of transitions—moving to a new city, switching careers, starting college, or even dealing with unexpected personal challenges. While change can feel intimidating, an optimistic mindset helps us see it as an opportunity rather than a setback.

As I mentioned in the previous chapter, I have experienced this firsthand when I had to switch schools multiple times. Each time, I found myself in a new environment, surrounded by unfamiliar faces, different teaching styles, and new challenges. It would have been easy to feel lost or resist the change, but instead, I chose to see it as a fresh start. With each transition, I learned to adapt, make new friends, and embrace different learning experiences. Looking back, those changes didn't hold me back—they helped me grow in ways I never expected.

As C.S. Lewis wisely said, "There are far, far better things ahead than any we leave behind." Life transitions may seem daunting, but with a hopeful outlook, they often lead to unexpected growth and new beginnings.

Cultural and Historical Inspiration: Lessons from the Past

History and mythology are filled with stories that remind us how optimism and perseverance can lead to victory, even in the face of adversity. Indian culture, in particular, is rich with such examples that continue to inspire generations.

One of the most powerful examples comes from The Ramayana. When Lord Rama was exiled from his kingdom and later faced the abduction of Sita by Ravana, he did not lose hope. Despite overwhelming odds, he remained determined, built alliances, and ultimately triumphed. His journey teaches us that challenges are inevitable, but with faith and persistence, one can overcome even the toughest situations.

Another great example is The Mahabharata, particularly the story of the Pandavas. After losing everything in a rigged game of dice, they could have succumbed to despair. Yet, instead of giving up, they used their years in exile to grow stronger, strategize, and ultimately reclaim their kingdom. Their belief in justice and their ability to rise again is a lesson in resilience and optimism.

Even in Indian history, we see such examples. Rani Lakshmibai, the queen of Jhansi, fought against the British during India's First War of Independence. Despite facing a far more powerful army, she refused to surrender, inspiring future generations with her courage and determination. Her story proves that even when the odds are against us, unwavering belief in oneself can lead to remarkable outcomes.

As Swami Vivekananda once said, "Arise, awake, and stop not till the goal is reached." Whether in mythology, history, or everyday life, optimism gives us the strength to keep moving forward, no matter how difficult the journey may seem.

Technological Impact: A Future Shaped by Optimism

Every major technological breakthrough in history started with someone who believed, this can be done. Without optimism, we wouldn't have electricity, the internet, or space exploration. The world's greatest inventors, scientists, and innovators all had one thing in common—they refused to be discouraged by failure.

Take the story of Dr. A.P.J. Abdul Kalam, India's "Missile Man." When he was leading India's space and missile programs, his first major project, the Satellite Launch Vehicle (SLV), failed in 1979. But instead of losing hope, he and his team analyzed what went wrong, worked harder, and the very next year, they successfully launched Rohini into space. His journey proves that setbacks are just stepping stones when seen through the lens of optimism.

On a smaller scale, optimism in technology isn't just about world-changing inventions—it's also about the patience and belief that small efforts add up over time. Many content creators start YouTube channels with enthusiasm, only to lose motivation when growth is slow. But those who persist, improving their content and learning from failures, often find success over time. Whether it's a budding filmmaker, an educator, or a tech enthusiast, their optimism fuels their progress even when results aren't immediate.

From self-driving cars to AI-driven healthcare, the future is being shaped by people who refuse to be discouraged by failures. As Elon Musk once said, "When something is important enough, you do it even if the odds are not in your favor." Technology thrives on optimism, and those who persist despite obstacles are the ones who eventually change the world.

Personal Growth: Becoming a Better Version of Yourself

Personal growth is a lifelong journey, and optimism plays a key role in shaping it. Whether it's developing a new skill, overcoming a fear, or working on self-discipline, an optimistic mindset helps us see progress as possible, even when the results are slow.

Take the story of Mary Kom, one of India's greatest boxers. Born in a small village, she faced countless challenges—financial struggles, societal expectations, and later, balancing motherhood with her career. Many would have given up, thinking their circumstances were too difficult to succeed. But Mary Kom believed in herself, trained relentlessly, and went on to become a world champion multiple times. Her story proves that growth isn't about having the perfect start; it's about having the mindset to keep going.

On a smaller scale, think about someone trying to build a habit—waking up early, practicing public speaking, or even learning to manage emotions better. Many give up after a few failed attempts, believing they'll never change. But those who approach personal growth with optimism, understanding that every effort counts, eventually transform themselves. As Carol Dweck, who pioneered the growth mindset concept, said, "Becoming is better than being." True growth happens when we believe that our efforts, no matter how small, will lead to a better version of ourselves.

Conclusion: The Many Faces of Optimism

In this chapter, I have tried to explore various dimensions of our daily lives where optimism plays an important role—whether it's in relationships, career aspirations, health, community engagement, or navigating major life transitions. It isn't just a mindset but a driving force that shapes our actions, fuels resilience, and helps us adapt to change. From history to modern-day innovations, from personal struggles to global movements, optimism has always been at the heart of progress.

Life beyond school is unpredictable, filled with twists we can't always control. But what we can control is how we respond. Through the examples we've explored, it's clear that optimism isn't about ignoring reality—it's about choosing to believe in possibilities, even when the road ahead looks uncertain. And sometimes, that belief is enough to turn the impossible into reality.

Reflection Activity: Practicing Optimism in Everyday Life

Over the next few days, try to consciously notice the little challenges you face in your daily life—whether it's a difficult homework assignment, an argument with a friend, or a plan that doesn't go as expected. Instead of reacting automatically, pause and ask yourself:

- How can I approach this situation with a more positive mindset?
- What is one small action I can take to make it better?
- Have I faced something similar before? How did I handle it then?
- What's one lesson I can take from this experience?

To make this more effective, keep a small journal or note on your phone where you jot down these moments. At the end of the week, look back and reflect—did shifting your mindset help? Did things turn out better than expected? The more you practice, the more natural optimism will become in your life, not just in school but in every challenge you face.

CHAPTER FIVE

Cultivating an Optimistic Mindset

"You have to be optimistic. I still have doubts and conflicts, but the bottom line is, I believe in the future."
— Frank Gehry

Let me ask you something: have you ever had a bad day that got worse just because of how you reacted to it? Like, you missed the bus, forgot your homework, and then told yourself, "This whole day is ruined." That's not the day – that's your mindset making it worse.

Meet Aanya.

Not a topper. Not failing either. Just... somewhere in the middle, trying to figure things out. One day, she got back her math test. 13 out of 25. Not great. Her friend beside her got a 23.

The old Aanya would've spiralled: "Ugh, I'm so dumb. Why can't I ever get it right? I should just give up."

But that day? She paused. Took a deep breath. And said to

herself: "Okay, I know exactly where I went wrong. This time, I'll fix it. I don't get it... *yet.*"

Was she instantly happy? Nope. But that one switch – from "I'm a failure" to "I'm learning" – changed everything. She asked for help after class. Watched a YouTube tutorial that night. Wrote down what confused her. Next test? She got 19. Not perfect, but progress.

Aanya's Mirror – React vs. Respond

Aanya could've reacted with frustration or self-hate, but she chose to respond with calm and clarity. Now it's your turn.

Think about your last "bad" day.

- Did you react with "Why is this happening to me?" or respond with "What can I do now?"
- What *one thought* made the day feel worse?

Write it down. Then rewrite it like Maya would:

- "This is hard" -> "This is hard *right now.*"
- "I always mess up" -> "I messed up this time. I'll learn from it."

See, optimism isn't magic. It's *mindset.* It's choosing to believe in *progress instead of perfection.*

The truth is, we all have those negative thoughts. But here's the cool part: *you don't have to believe everything your brain says.* Seriously. *A thought is not a fact.*

Optimism isn't about being blindly positive all the time. It's about saying, "Okay, things went wrong... but what now?" It's about training your brain to bounce back, to choose solutions over spirals.

In this chapter, we'll explore how to stop being your own worst critic, how to rewire those automatic negative thoughts, and how to build habits that make optimism your second nature.

Ready to shift your mindset like a boss? Let's go.

It begins in tiny, almost innocent ways.

Maybe you study hard for a test but end up with a disappointing mark. Disappointment? Totally normal. But instead of just feeling it and moving forward, your mind takes a dangerous shortcut:

"I'm not smart enough."

You scroll through Instagram later that evening, seeing classmates at events you weren't invited to, awards ceremonies you weren't a part of, and vacations you can't afford. Without consciously choosing to, you think:

"Everyone is ahead of me. I'm falling behind."

Here's the thing — none of these moments are life-shattering. On their own, they're just small bumps.

But our brains are wired to stitch these moments together into a story — and if that story is repeated often enough, it becomes our personal reality.

This is where negativity starts digging in — not as a fleeting feeling, but as a mental loop your mind practices daily. Over time, it doesn't feel like a story anymore. It feels like truth.

The Science Behind It: Why Our Brain Clings to Negativity

You're not broken for thinking this way. You're human.

Our brains are designed with something called *Negativity Bias* — a tendency to focus more on negative experiences than positive ones. It's not a flaw. It's evolutionary. Thousands of years ago, survival meant being alert to threats. If our ancestors ignored a warning sound in the forest — a snapping twig, a growl — they risked their lives. So the brain evolved to prioritize bad news over good news.

Today, there's no tiger behind the bushes. But your brain still treats criticism from a teacher or a failed project like it's a mortal danger. That one negative comment sticks far more firmly than ten compliments.

And thanks to *neuroplasticity* — the brain's ability to rewire itself — the more you entertain negative thoughts, the stronger the connections between those thoughts become.

Imagine a small footpath in a forest. The more you walk on it, the clearer and wider it gets. Eventually, it becomes a highway.

In the same way, repeated negative thinking builds highways in your brain — until negativity becomes the automatic route your mind takes.

From Habit to Belief: The Real Danger

Once negativity becomes a habit, it doesn't stay contained. It seeps deeper and transforms into beliefs — quiet, stubborn convictions about who you are and how life works.

It's subtle at first.

You get one bad grade and think, "Maybe I'm not good at math."

Fail a tryout, and you mumble, "Maybe I'm not meant for sports."

Lose a friendship, and whisper, "Maybe I'm just hard to love."

These beliefs seem harmless, but over time, they start shaping your behavior.

The student who believes they are "bad at speaking" stops volunteering for presentations.

The teenager who thinks they are "bad at sports" avoids practice sessions.

The person who believes they're "not lovable" pulls away from friends.

Beliefs become a *self-fulfilling prophecy*.

They're not just thoughts anymore — they become the lens through which you view every experience. You interpret the world not as it is, but through the distorted mirror of what you've been conditioned to believe about yourself.

And unless challenged, these beliefs dig their roots so deep that even positive experiences struggle to dislodge them.

Spotting the Negativity Trap

Spotting the negativity trap is about becoming aware of how subtle the process is. It often begins with small, seemingly harmless thoughts:

"I could have done better."

"Everyone else seems happier than me."

"Maybe I'm just not meant for this."

Individually, these thoughts don't seem dangerous. In fact, they can feel justified. After all, everyone gets disappointed, right? But the trap lies not in a single bad day or a single moment of doubt — it lies in the pattern. When thoughts like these become the default background music of your life, you're caught in the trap.

Signs you're slipping into the negativity trap:

-You mentally rehearse your mistakes far more than your victories.

-You downplay compliments but replay criticism on a loop.
-You expect things to go wrong, even before they do.
-You compare your worst moments to others' highlight reels (hello, Instagram scroll).

The key to spotting the trap is *self-awareness*.

When a negative thought pops up, pause and ask yourself: "Is this thought a fact, or just a feeling?" "Am I reacting to a single event, or building a whole story around it?"

The moment you start questioning your thoughts instead of blindly believing them, you loosen the trap's hold. Because thoughts are powerful — but only if we accept them as truth without checking if they deserve that power.

When Negative Thoughts Attack

Let's be real: even when you know all about the negativity trap, there will be days when negative thoughts hit you like an unexpected storm.

Maybe you flunked a test you thought you'd ace. Maybe you had a fight with a friend. Maybe you just woke up feeling off for no obvious reason.

Negative thoughts are tricky — they're like fast-moving shadows. They don't wait for permission. They show up in the middle of your most vulnerable moments.

And when they attack, they feel real. They feel urgent. They feel true.

<u>**Here's how negative thoughts usually attack**</u>:

1. <u>They Sound Like Your Own Voice:</u>
   Not a villainous whisper. Just your regular inner voice, casually saying things like:
   "You're not good enough."

"Why even try?"

"Everyone else is doing better."

Because it sounds like you, it's easy to trust it. But remember: just because a thought sounds convincing doesn't mean it is the truth.

2. <u>They Use Absolutes</u>:

Words like "always," "never," "everyone," "no one."

"I always mess up."

"No one cares."

"Nothing ever works out for me."

Absolutes are red flags. Real life isn't black-and-white like that. When you hear yourself using extreme words, it's a sign that negativity is trying to control the narrative.

3. <u>They Make You Feel Stuck</u>:

Negative thoughts don't usually lead to solutions. They lead to paralysis. Instead of motivating you to fix things, they drag you deeper into hopelessness.

You replay mistakes. You predict failures. You feel like nothing you do will matter anyway.

So what can you actually do when negativity attacks?

- <u>Name the Thought</u>:

Literally call it out.

"This is a negative thought trying to hijack my mind."

Naming it reminds you: this is a thought, not an identity.

- <u>Challenge It</u>:

Ask:

"Is there real evidence for this?"

"What would I tell a friend if they were thinking this?"
(You'd never tell a friend they were worthless for failing
a test. Don't accept it from yourself.)

- Shift the Focus:
  If you can't immediately flip the thought (and
  sometimes you can't), shift your attention. Move your
  body. Change your environment. Call someone you
  trust. Take one tiny productive step. Even a small action
  loosens negativity's grip.

- Breathe and Delay:
  Negative thoughts thrive on urgency.
  "You're failing. Fix it now!"
  "You're a loser. Do something drastic!"
  Delay reacting. Breathe. Give yourself permission to feel
  bad for a moment without making big decisions. Most
  storms blow over faster than they feel in the moment.

Recognizing negativity when it strikes is *powerful* — but
recognizing alone isn't *enough*.
If you keep living in the same mental environment,
negativity will keep finding you.
You see, negativity feeds on certain conditions:
comparison, isolation, burnout, self-doubt.
If those conditions remain, it doesn't matter how many
times you fight a negative thought — another one will soon
take its place.

That's why true growth begins when you don't just react to negativity, but build an environment where positivity has the upper hand.

Think of it like this:
Imagine you're trying to stay dry in a rainstorm.
You can keep dodging raindrops one by one... or you can build a solid shelter.
Negativity will always exist — in the world, in people, sometimes even in you.
But the shelter you build — through habits, through your surroundings, through the people you trust — will decide how much it touches you.

Building your shield is not about pretending life is perfect.
It's about preparing your mind and your space so that when negativity attacks, you're already two steps ahead.
You're not scrambling to protect yourself — you're standing strong because your foundation was built wisely, intentionally, and with hope at the center.

Now, let's talk about how to build that shield:
Through your environment, your habits, your mindset — and simple but powerful tools that, over time, will rewire the way you experience life itself.

You don't just spot the negativity trap anymore.
You outgrow it.

The following tools and techniques are timeless practices, rooted both in ancient wisdom and cutting-edge psychology, designed to guide you towards a life anchored in positivity and growth.

1. Curate Your Inputs: Guard Your Mind Like a Gatekeeper

Your mind becomes what you feed it. In today's hyper-connected world, the content you consume—news, social media, conversations—shapes your emotions and beliefs.

-Be intentional:

Surround yourself with positive people who uplift and inspire you.

Choose educational, empowering media over fear-driven or negative content.

-Limit doom-scrolling and create a "Positive Playlist" of books, podcasts, videos, and articles that nurture optimism.

-Corporate parallel: In business, leaders don't entertain all data equally—they prioritize high-quality inputs. Treat your mind the same way.

2. Celebrate Small Wins: Build a Habit of Micro-Success

Success is not one giant leap—it's a series of small, seemingly insignificant victories.

By acknowledging small wins daily, you wire your brain to notice progress rather than problems.

-Check tasks off a to-do list, however small.

-Take a moment to feel proud after completing even a minor challenge.

Pro tip: Create a "Wins Journal" where you list 3 things you accomplished each day. This technique rewires your brain for achievement and gratitude simultaneously.

3. Practice Gratitude: The Oldest, Most Powerful Life Hack

Gratitude shifts your focus from what's lacking to what's abundant. It's a simple yet revolutionary practice.

-Each morning, write down three things you are grateful for.

-Before sleeping, reflect on a good moment from the day.

-Say "thank you" genuinely to people around you.

Remember: Gratitude isn't ignoring challenges—it's choosing to see blessings despite challenges.

4. Progress Over Perfection: Excellence, Not Perfectionism

Perfectionism is the enemy of growth. Striving for "perfect" paralyzes action and creates fear of failure.

Instead, embrace progress:

-Focus on effort and learning, not flawless outcomes.

-Treat mistakes as feedback, not final verdicts.

-Repeat after me: "Done is better than perfect."

Be a lifelong learner, not a one-time achiever.

5. Positive Self-Talk: Become Your Own Biggest Cheerleader

The way you talk to yourself matters more than you realize. Negative self-talk plants seeds of doubt and defeat; positive self-talk builds strength and self-esteem.

Upgrade your inner dialogue:

-Replace "I can't do this" with "I'm learning how to do this."

-Shift from "I failed" to "I grew."

-Formal exercise: Every time you catch a negative thought, consciously reframe it into a supportive one.

6. Experience Random Moments of Positivity

Positivity doesn't always come scheduled. Seek it spontaneously:

-Watch a funny video when you feel stuck.

-Compliment a stranger.

-Share a laugh with a friend.

These tiny injections of joy are powerful—they're like mini-breaks for your mental health.

7. Randomly Smile: Trick Your Brain (In the Best Way)

This might sound simple, but research backs it: smiling—even when you don't feel like it—boosts serotonin and dopamine (the happiness chemicals).

-Start your day by smiling at yourself in the mirror.

-Smile randomly when walking, sitting, or thinking.

Smiling is a free mood booster. It's basic biology at play. Use it to your advantage.

8. Journaling: Your Private Power Tool

Journaling is not just for writers—it's for anyone who values mental clarity and emotional growth.

Daily or weekly, write freely about:

-What's on your mind

-What you learned

-What you're grateful for

-What dreams you are nurturing

Journaling gives your emotions a safe space and helps you notice patterns in your thinking.

9. Self-Care: You Cannot Pour From An Empty Cup

Self-care is not selfish—it's strategic.

Prioritize physical, emotional, and spiritual wellbeing:
-Sleep adequately.
-Eat nourishing food.
-Move your body regularly.
-Take tech-breaks to reconnect with yourself.
Protect your most valuable asset. In life, your asset is YOU.

10. Meditation and Mindfulness: Reboot Your Mental Software

Meditation is ancient technology designed for the modern mind. Even 5–10 minutes a day can:
-Reduce stress
-Enhance concentration
-Strengthen emotional resilience

Simple practices to begin:
-Focus on your breath for one minute.
-Do a body scan to notice where you hold tension.
-Practice "mindful walking," where you simply observe each step and breath.
Pro Tip: Consistency beats intensity. Short daily meditation is more effective than occasional long sessions.

Conclusion: You Are The Architect of Your Mind

At the end of the day, mindset is a choice you renew every moment.

It is not about being endlessly cheerful or pretending problems don't exist—it's about choosing hope, effort, and growth over despair and stagnation.

Positivity is not an emotion; it is a skill—a muscle—a way of life.

Remember:
You don't have to control everything.

You just have to master yourself.
And every small, imperfect, positive step you take shapes the future you are building.

44

Conclusion

And just like that, we're here — at the last page.

First of all, thank you. Thank you for choosing to spend your precious time reading what is honestly just a piece of my heart spilled into words.

This isn't a typical "book-book" filled with complicated theories or heavy advice. It's simply what I've lived, felt, questioned, and explored — and what I believed was worth sharing with you.

Writing The Optimistic Teen at this stage of my life has been more than just putting sentences together. It's been about capturing the spirit of growing up — the confusion, the excitement, the doubt, the hope. It's about understanding that while life isn't always perfect, our attitude can be our superpower.

If there's one thing I want you to take from this, it's that being optimistic doesn't mean having all the answers. It doesn't mean pretending everything's fine when it's not. It means *believing* that even when things get tough — you have it in you to get through it. It means trusting that small steps count. That setbacks are part of the plan. That dreams are never too big if you have the heart to chase them.

I'm truly grateful to everyone who encouraged me to write, who supported me silently, who gave feedback (good or bad) — because every bit helped me become better.

This book is just the beginning. Our stories are still being written, one day at a time. So stay hopeful. Stay hungry to grow. Stay brave enough to dream bigger than people expect you to.

And hey — if you ever feel like sharing your thoughts, ideas, or even just saying hi, I'd absolutely love to hear from you. You can reach me at virikagarg2203@gmail.com .

Thank you again, from the bottom of my heart.

Keep believing. Keep building. The future belongs to dreamers who dare to stay optimistic.